To David and to Lucy
with love

This edition is published by special arrangement with Margaret K. McElderry Books, an imprint of Macmillan Publishing Company.

Grateful acknowledgment is made to Margaret K. McElderry Books, an imprint of Macmillan Publishing Company for permission to reprint *Dear Mr. Blueberry* by Simon James. Copyright © 1991 by Simon James.

Printed in Mexico

ISBN 0-15-302136-5

4 5 6 7 8 9 10   050   97 96 95

Dear Mr. Blueberry

SIMON JAMES

HARCOURT BRACE & COMPANY

Orlando Atlanta Austin Boston San Francisco Chicago Dallas New York
Toronto London

Dear Mr. Blueberry,

I love whales very much and I think I saw one in my pond today. Please send me some information on whales, as I think he might be hurt.

Love
Emily

Dear Emily,

Here are some details about whales. I don't think you'll find it was a whale you saw, because whales don't live in ponds, but in salt water.

Yours sincerely
Your teacher,

Mr. Blueberry

Dear Mr. Blueberry,

  I am now putting salt into the pond every day before breakfast and last night I saw my whale smile. I think he is feeling better.

  Do you think he might be lost?

Love
Emily

Dear Emily,

   Please don't put any more salt
in the pond. I'm sure your parents
won't be pleased.

   I'm afraid there can't be a whale
in your pond, because whales don't
get lost, they always know where
they are in the oceans.

      Yours sincerely,

        Mr. Blueberry

Dear Mr. Blueberry,

Tonight I am very happy because I saw my whale jump up and spurt lots of water. He looked blue.

Does this mean he might be a blue whale?

Love
Emily

P.S. What can I feed him with?

Dear Emily,

Blue whales are blue and they eat tiny shrimplike creatures that live in the sea. However, I must tell you that a blue whale is much too big to live in your pond.

Yours sincerely,

Mr. Blueberry

P.S. Perhaps it is a blue goldfish?

Dear Mr. Blueberry,

   Last night I read your letter to my whale. Afterward he let me stroke his head. It was very exciting.

   I secretly took him some crunched-up cornflakes and bread crumbs. This morning I looked in the pond and they were all gone!

   I think I shall call him Arthur. What do you think?

Love
Emily

Dear Emily,

I must point out to you quite forcibly now that in no way could a whale live in your pond. You may not know that whales are migratory, which means they travel great distances each day.

I am sorry to disappoint you.

Yours sincerely,

Mr. Blueberry

Dear Mr. Blueberry,

   Tonight I'm a little sad. Arthur has gone. I think your letter made sense to him and he has decided to be migratory again.

Love
Emily

Dear Emily,

Please don't be too sad, it really was impossible for a whale to live in your pond. Perhaps when you are older you would like to sail the oceans studying and protecting whales.

Yours sincerely,

Mr. Blueberry

Dear Mr. Blueberry,

It's been the happiest day!
I went to the beach and you'll
never guess, but I saw Arthur!
I called to him and he smiled.
I knew it was Arthur because
he let me stroke his head.

I gave him some of my
sandwich . . .

and then we said good-bye.

   I shouted that I loved him very much and, I hope you don't mind, I said you loved him, too.

Love
   Emily (and Arthur)

The End